Excalibur's Return

Also by Maurice Whelan

Non-fiction

Special Education and Social Control: Invisible Disasters
Mistress of Her Own Thoughts: Ella Freeman Sharpe
In the Company of William Hazlitt

Fiction

Boat People

Poetry

The Lilac Bow

Maurice Whelan

Excalibur's Return

Maurice Whelan
Dec 2011

Acknowledgements

'Snowdrop Moon' was first published in *Revival* in October 2010.

I am grateful to countless people who have taken the time to read my poems.
I am particularly indebted to the following:
Lena Bruselid, Gary Bryson, Ian Colley, Alison Craswell, Michael Dudley,
Judy Griffiths, Winton Higgins, Richard O'Neill-Dean, Stuart Rees,
Lorraine Rose, Ella Whelan, Louise Whelan, Bob White.
Their comments and criticisms have improved my writing;
its failings are my own.

My thanks to Tom Griffiths for use of the cover image.

My continuing thanks to Stephen Matthews for publishing my work.

Excalibur's Return
ISBN 978 1 74027 693 1
Copyright © text Maurice Whelan 2011

First published 2011 by
GINNINDERRA PRESS
PO Box 3461 Port Adelaide SA 5015
www.ginninderrapress.com.au

Contents

Snowdrop Moon	9
Dawn in Willoughby	10
Morning at Curl Curl	11
Excalibur's Return	12
Little Wonders	13
Farm Work	14
Big Brother	16
Water Falls	17
Wise Man	18
Zero Zero One One	19
Ugly Duckling	21
Anglo Irish	22
After Shock	24
Juicy Fruit	26
Fairweather Man	27
Departed Virtue	28
Mount Cargill	29
My Father	30
Magic Mountain	33
Real Presence	35
Perpendicular	36
Perfect Pitch	37
In a Spin	38
Stardust	39
Gentle Messenger	40
Mirror Image	41
Falling Water	42
Offering a Poem to be Read	43
Bad Language	45
Love	46
Parting Glance	47
Dark Moon	48
Afterword	49

To Richard
at whose side I ran up Mount Cargill

My mind to me a kingdom is,
Such perfect joy therein I find,
That it excels all other bliss
That earth affords or grows by kind.

Edward Dyer (1550–1607)

Poetry…is not a branch of authorship: it is 'the stuff of which our life is made' all that is worth remembering in life, is the poetry of it… Poetry is that fine particle within us, that expands, rarefies, refines, raises our whole being: without it 'man's life is poor as beast's'.

William Hazlitt (1778–1830)

Snowdrop Moon

High in the night sky
a full low-sheen moon
glows in the light
of the hidden sun.

Down under a leafy canopy
a silent snowdrop
bends its face
to the earth.

On the tip of each
pure white petal
nature's paintbrush
paints a fleck of green.

A tiny lantern
offering beauty and light
unchanged by night
and winter's darkness.

Dawn in Willoughby

6 a.m. Mowbray Road, Sydney 3 February 2009

The sun angles itself
under a wide bank of thin cloud
a huge pink fan
like a giant hanger
leans over the suburb
fresh and new.

'Tis dangerous
to look away
it holds
its perfection
as long
as you hold your breath.

Morning at Curl Curl

With thanks to William Shakespeare

There is no line to separate
sea and sky
liquid silver light
upon the surface of the water
dances into the air
takes the breath away
almost dazzles.

From fathoms deep
Prospero's broken staff
has mended
and his drowned book
which was cast
'deeper than did ever plummet sound'
has risen
new spells have been released
airy charms sing their magic
on that great stage
between the waters and the skies.

Excalibur's Return

It hasn't rained for weeks.
Lane Cove River is like a pond
the unseen sun
peels shadows
from the trees
silken pillars rest
upon the surface of the water.

From such stillness
wonders are born
from water such as this
Tennyson's magic maiden's arm
'clothed in white samite, mystic, wonderful,'
rose with King Arthur's sword Excalibur.

Close your eyes.
See the surface of your soul
part clean and dry
the jewels of your nightfall
the poetry of your dreams
mystic moments of your past
will rise and shine and reach
beyond your half-forgotten days.

Little Wonders

Small shells sand and stones
gathered from beaches mountains
and riverbeds across the world
sit on the window sill.

One stone bears my mark
'Achill 88' recalls a lobster meal
the Citroen 2CV's wiper
blades battling
Atlantic mist and rain.

Jewels of the earth in pristine exile
glowing glistening gliding
through the mountains and the seas
and the river beds of my remembrance.

Farm Work

There was drudgery in the work.
Those cold damp days
when you drove
the Ferguson up and down up
and down the field
the grey tractor half losing itself
in the lingering morning fog
the mowing bar
making straight rows
of the felled peas.

I stood at the headland tidying
rescuing the small stray green stalks
from the large wheels
my fingers like icicles
gripping the wooden pitchfork handle

my nose dripping
praying for rain
to go indoors
leave the soggy socks
and the leaden boots scattered
on the scullery floor.

Stand beside you
backs to the Aga
the steam rising
from our bodies
answering mother's fear –
you'll catch your death –
silently
defiantly
claiming
worker status.

Now the misery is remembered.
So is the precious bond with you
my fellow worker
my brother.

Big Brother

I was thirteen he was three years older
we sat at the table in an Irish farmhouse
doing our homework.

No wooden shelves heavy
with the tomes of the ages.
We had orange crates
made from balsa wood
bound by thin strands of wire
turned on their side.

Inside this flimsy structure
Stood our books: Irish English
Latin history geography
science religion arithmetic
algebra geometry –
wisdom waiting
behind faded burgundy spines.

We worked in silence
until the time came
to learn by rote
great reams of Shakespeare
mutterings and murmurings
intermingling his Hamlet saying
'What a piece of work is man,'
my Mark Anthony declaring he had
'Come to bury Caesar, not to praise him.'

We few, we happy few,
we band of brothers.

Water Falls

In the Blue Mountains
between Govett's Leap
and Evans Lookout
under the well-constructed
wooden footbridge
a small stream passes
on a gentle gradient
going
it knows not where.

Further along the track
it emerges
where the escarpment
a wall of sandstone
drops a hundred metres
or more.

From burbling liquid
swaying into every nook
and cranny gravity permits
it has become a waterfall
a spray
translucent
spinning and tossing and twisting itself
through the air
like a smiling trapeze artist
descending on invisible wires
plunging
like a bungee jumper
rising
in languid merriment
confident in the promise
that when it ceases
to be airborne
it will once again
return to its old self.

Wise Man

John McGahern wrote in his Memoir

'...it is from those days
that I take the belief
that the best of life
is life lived quietly,
where nothing happens
but our calm progress
through the day,
where change is imperceptible
and the precious life
is everything.'

That should be a poem!

Zero Zero One One

Clock tells twenty-five past six
sun freshens pink and white azaleas
outside the window
mug of camomile tea steams
on my desk
like a small monument
the telephone waits
zero zero one one
three five three…
and onwards

My mind swifter than
the speed of light swifter than
radio waves watches you
at your kitchen table.

I see you turning your eyes
observing the slim grey object
as if you were seeing it
for the first time
as if it was that large black phone
with the round dial
and a handle at the side
installed in the farmhouse
fifty years ago
a noisy intrusion
into an ancient world.

It will ring seven times
before you say your hesitant
'Hellooo,'
and, 'Oh, it's you, son,'
as you smile and your voice swiftly
rises and softens into a whispering song.

When you hear my first words
you marvel as you always do
at the clarity of the voice
making its long journey
from the other side of the world.

'Ten thousand miles!
All the way from Australia!
The line is sooo clear.
Sure you could just
be over in Shangana.'

Ugly Duckling

1 March 2009, Glenbrook New South Wales

Clinging to the cliff face
its roots like gnarled knuckles
an old man's fist
pressed upon a rock
callused fingers and deformed joints
elongated
knobbly
warts and growths
in profusion

pink
pale-grey
rusty-coloured bark
angophora costata
a remarkable beauty
patiently awaits appreciation.

Anglo Irish

I never learned the Gaelic tongue
with any fluency but of late
long-forgotten words
old songs
poems
visit in the night.

Deep inside me the poem-songs sing
like summer leaves shimmering in the trees
like autumn leaves rustling under my feet.

Cad a dhéanfaimid feasta gan adhmad?
Tá deireadh na gcoillte ar lár;
níl trácht ar Chill Cháis ná ar a teaghlach
is ní bainfear a cling go bráth.

Thomas Kinsella translated the Gaelic
words of the unknown bard:
Now what will we do for timber,
with the last of the woods laid low?
There's no talk of Kilcash or its household
and its bell will be struck no more.

Lost words lost worlds
one and the same
languages like tall trees
drive roots
deep into the soil of the mind
the silent bell tolls for the silent voice.

One man's gibberish
is to another's ear
sweet music
the score
written in his mother's eyes
her voice the bow
that moves from string to string.

Melodies now wander
in the twilight of my mind
calling me
to the dawn
to my creation
the moments when sounds
sang their way
into the marrow
of my soul.

After Shock

Small thin poor
clean-shaven to a fault
cloth cap pulled over watery eyes
in a sleepy Irish town
1956
he leans against the wall
of the corner shop
head and neck
twitching twisting twitching
muttering words
words
the world can't wait
to listen for.

Shells fired at the Somme
forty years away
seek the ground
he stands upon
the stench of rotting corpse
infests the fabric of his skin
night and day
cannons
pound inside his skull.

From that Second Great War
to end all wars
from Vietnam Iraq Afghanistan
bombs seek all corners
of this sunburnt land
night and day
day and night
they detonate
shatter the mind
behind the eyes
muttering watery words
words
our world can't wait
to listen for.

Juicy Fruit

Cezanne's still life
fruit bowls
were irresistible.

When the crowd thinned
he grasped
his moment.

Lip-smacking
mouth-watering
amazing.

Fairweather Man

On a home-made raft
a latter-day Jonah

cast himself adrift
in the Timor Sea

floated
on the soft belly of the earth

swallowed
by the void

found
by favourable winds

he returned
restored

refreshed our eyes
with sights unseen.

Departed Virtue

In the midst of the bustling crowd
Jesus said
who touched me

and the woman
with the issue of blood
confessed
she stole his virtue.

How do we know
who takes

and who is moved
by a delicate
need
for grace?

Mount Cargill

'It's snowing here,' you said. 'Do you remember
the day we ran up Mount Cargill?'
'The day we ran up Mount Cargill
is as fresh in my mind
as yesterday
as your voice,'
I answered,
'and I can see the snow on the car
windscreen as we drove to the foot
of the mountain the swishing blades
like a plasterer's trowel
skimming the surface clean.'

We broke into a trot
fresh-fallen snow
squelched and squished
under our feet like a softened drum roll
on the mountain's white skin.

I the seasoned distance runner
you the veteran of Everest
together we wound round and up
Mount Cargill
feeling like kings
glowing in the light
and the shadow
of each other.

My Father

He listened to Beethoven
learned German from
Linguaphone records
crawled on his hands
and knees
between the beet drills
glanced over his shoulder
turned his eyes back to the earth.

I stood on the headland
wrapped the sacking around my legs
and followed in the drill beside him
and I sat in the rarely-used sitting room
with the smell of paraffin heaters
watched his shy smile
closed my eyes and heard him sing
'Danny Boy' and 'I Will Take You Home Again, Kathleen'
and always
almost cried.

Never did he raise a hand
or voice in anger
but I hated the sullen silence
that gripped his soul
placed him beyond my reach
beyond my power of speech.

Filial duty had bound him
to the land
he had hopes
I could place my feet
upon a higher ground.

And so it came to pass
I followed in the slipstream of his dreams
not knowing
where it had begun
how it would end
I became a wanderer
between Alpha and Omega.

When his end drew near
I travelled home
too weak to lift his head
with faltering voice he asked
what did life add up to
he who had certainty under his belt
he whose God had watched his every move
a sparrow's flight never fails
without being known.

I held his hand
told him all I knew
all I did not know
all I could bear to say
the only certainty
this was my last time at his side.

For all too brief a time
our spirits walked together
in a new dream
in the footprints
of an invisible silence.

It was the first time
he had asked the big question
the first time he said
the answer was beyond him
the first time he listened
to my answer
such as it was.

Life with all its brutal power
condemns words to death.

Death with all its brutal power
breaks the strangle hold of silence.

Magic Mountain

For Eric, Linda and Louise

Last year we walked
on the rim of the Blue Mountains
from Gordon Falls to Leura Cascades.
As far as the eye could see
the green of a thousand trees
met the blue of a limitless sky
ancient escarpments
kissed by the sun
the Bridal Veil Falls
shivered
silver and white.

Today at every lookout
dense fog
like a giant cloud
fills the valley.

If someone said
the end of the world has come
if someone said
the Milky Way is visiting
the Blue Mountains
I'd say wonders never cease.

'Look up,' one of us called.
'It's like a Chinese painting.'
Branches merge with mist
silver leaves
clothed in fine silk
on invisible threads
hang from the heavens
twigs like pencil marks
on a draftsman's page
pale-grey light-green
fade into whiteness.

Real Presence

Your spirit at my side
absent footprints
in the snow.

Perpendicular

He stumbled and surveyed
the wreck
the wreckage that was his life

wasted years
dreams paralysed
love extinguished.

Hope flickered
arid soil turned to green
grey skies to blue

storm wind to gentle breeze
scent of lilac and of roses made
a prodigal's return.

Years have passed
the ground beneath his feet still
grants asylum

and every now and then
when misadventure or misfortune
lean their shadows

on his failings he stands tall
says I am done with weeping
walks steadily on.

Perfect Pitch

It happened impromptu
when the word impromptu
was beyond me.
People would call to the house
there'd be talk
of the weather
of rheumatism and lumbago
of who had died
and who had lately
come into the world.

The violin case would open
the melodeon taken from its box
tin whistles from the shelf.
Speech would cease.
Eyes close
and voices turn to song.

That was fifty years ago.
And today
I wait in silence and when I hear
the perfect pitch of stillness
I know the bow is on the string
fingers caress the keys, eyes
are closing and heaven's gate
is opening once again.

In a Spin

Three thousand light years
from earth
two pulsars spin
a dizzy path in a perpetual dance

The leader turns
every 2.7 seconds
his partner every 22 milliseconds
they circle each other
in 2.5 earth hours.

Like flashing lighthouses
they beam waves
across the Milky Way.
In 85 million years
their courtship will end
with collision.

I can't wait for the sight
of their final union.

Stardust

On hearing Martin Hayes play the fiddle

Words
      like your musical notes
      refuse to be bound
      by written score
      they dance from the page
      leap across the sky
      like a comet's tail
      streak beyond the horizon
      of my inward ear.

My pen
      a net
      to reach into the nebulae
      to catch the dust
      of collapsing stars
awaits its obedience.

On the train
crossing the Harbour Bridge
I look back at the Opera House
on the white envelope
that held the tickets
to masters of tradition
I scribble
this.

Gentle Messenger

Radio waves from the Big Bang
travel to planet earth
their energy
a fraction
of a falling
snowflake.

Reach out and touch
reach out and be touched
by this gentle messenger
from the beginning of time.

Mirror Image

Don't look away
I wasn't staring.
I saw my youth in you.

That's all.

Falling Water

Days and days of rain
and the once-dry rock face
plays host to a waterfall.

Silver-white
liquid gold
I welcome you.

Offering a Poem to be Read

It was the first time another person's
eyes looked upon that page
that assemblage of words
black on white
a short poem
twenty seconds at the most
of reading.

It was many multiples
of twenty seconds in the making.

Conception can occur
in a variety of ways
I can't remember how that one began
or when I knew it was finished
it must have hitched a ride
on my unconscious
made a place for itself
without asking
my ego's by your leave
could have been there for years
until all of a sudden
it steps into the light of day.

After that the making
takes an hour
a day a week a year
sometimes longer
it can be mind-breaking work
blood sweat and tears extended
to craft simple words
mould them
into a written spoken
miniature
work of art.

Twenty seconds
do me the honour
of reading it twice
while I craft for the eye
I compose for the ear
so read at least once
out loud.
Please.

Bad Language

If I was nice and polite
I'd say that writing
is always an inspired affair
I stare at the stars await the muse
and gentle reader
on the wings of poesy
words float to my pen
and mysteriously imprint the page.

If I was less than nice and polite
I would say that writing can be
bloody back-breaking
bone-crunching body-numbing
brain-shrinking work.

Sometimes finding the right word
is like drilling through concrete
with a jack hammer
to knock a sentence into shape
I beat it like a blacksmith
striking hot iron on an anvil.

Sometimes words and phrases like wild beasts
dig deep into their lairs
dragged out kicking and screaming
my alphabetical wonder stands before me
like a rabbit in a high beam
I breathe a sigh of relief
it leaps into the night
the space it vacates remains
mocks my dumb impudence.
Sure 'tis nothing short of a miracle
that anything half-decent* ever got wrote.

*If you honour me and read this one again, you might like to know that
on an Irish peasant's tongue, 'decent' would sound 'day-sent'.

Love

The evening sunbeams
strike the still surface of the lake

leap like dancers
from the mirrored waters

wrap their shimmering forms
around the ghost gums

cool flames of liquid light
caress the smooth grey-white bark

love
hungry for beauty.

Parting Glance

Upon the western horizon
the sun
a yellow dome
lingers
rays of light
steal under the foliage
to illuminate the trunks
of angophoras and red gums.

Without the painter's skill
to capture and to hold
I imagine tracing paper
pressed upon the forest
simple pencil strokes
brushed across the surface
the dark and the light
the peace and the silent
remnants of the day –
my masterpiece.

Dark Moon

Rising while the house sleeps
staring through the window pane
dark vestments
rest upon the shoulders
of the world.

Grass and trees
flowers and seas
have lost their colour.

I wait to witness
the daily birth
of light.

Afterword

The title of this collection is inspired by Alfred Tennyson's *Morte D'Arthur*. In that poem, King Arthur tells how he received his sword Excalibur from the maiden in the lake.

> In those old days, one summer noon, an arm
> Rose up from out the bosom of the lake,
> Clothed in white samite, mystic, wonderful,
> Holding the sword – and how I row'd across
> And took it, and have worn it, like a king.

Fifty years ago as a schoolboy, I first read that poem and learned large sections of it by heart. Then for decades I forgot about it until one day, browsing in a second-hand bookshop, I found an old anthology of English poetry. When I read the first line, the words and the music of the poem flooded back. I could close my eyes and reliably recite a whole page.

The Irish poet Rupert Strong said that the poet picks up a bow and sends an arrow back through the centuries. In the bookshop an arrow that had been launched in my childhood and disappeared from view – as if behind a cloud – had made an appearance once again. And with it came that same sense of childlike wonder and mystification. Wonder at how simple words could paint such beautiful scenes. Mystification at the fine music that language plays on human heartstrings

Poetry is no respecter of time or place. That is one of its great strengths. In the summer of 2008 I was in Lane Cove Park in Sydney looking down on the river and when I imagined Tennyson's magic maiden rising from the still waters, I wrote the title poem of this collection.

The capacity to be still is one of the most precious qualities in life. In today's world where frenzied communication is god, it is a rare commodity. Many of the poems in this collection address issues of stillness and silence. So it is not surprising that nature in its many manifestations figures prominently – from the tiny snowdrop at our feet to the pulsar millions of light years away. Even with the poem 'After Shock', which deals with the destructive effect of war, it is the absence of stillness and the impossibility of silence inside the mind of the traumatised soldier that is most damaging.

The tone of this volume is set by Edward Dyer and William Hazlitt. To them, poetry was an internal life force; that fine particle within us, as Hazlitt says, that lifts our whole being. Dyer encourages us to treat our minds, and the space within us where self-consciousness resides, as a kingdom.

When you can live with silence and stillness, your words find a hidden key, and everything you hear and speak changes. Stillness isn't a static place where nothing happens. Silence makes room for imagination, inspiration and the capacity to listen.

The shortest poem here is a few lines, the longest a few pages. Each attempts to capture an atmosphere. Many draw on deeply personal experience. But the personal only has relevance if it wanders into the experience of others, dovetails with that experience and draws strength from it. Therefore, a poem's success rests entirely on whether it can be called a piece of art. I hope I am not being pretentious in making that claim, but that is how I judge the poems. When I consider them deserving of that status, they are ready to leave me and enter the public domain. (My notebooks are full of others which have failed the test.) A poem is a piece of art if it allows you to take it into yourself. As James Joyce said, a piano is a coffin of notes that requires a pianist to play it. John McGahern added that a book is a coffin of words that requires a reader to bring it to life.

Stillness is a condition that promotes privacy. Privacy is another precious commodity that in today's world is under rapacious assault. (A metaphor of biblical allusion is appropriate here. Privacy is a pearl of great price that is often traded as worthless.) Fiction – poetry, short stories and the novel – are great defenders of privacy. If the writer has done his work and created that piece of art, he should glide into the shadows and leave the reader free, in the privacy of his own mind, to imagine things that are exclusively his. Good fiction writers are never instructive. They are present, but at an intimately respectful distance. The artist, according to Flaubert, should not appear any more in his work than God in nature: present everywhere, but nowhere visible.

The artist needs a childlike innocence, a natural trust that his inner nature will guide him. 'An artist,' according to the English writer Charles Morgan, 'is a child who stares.' Morgan's description of childish wonder is poetry itself.

> Have you ever watched a child, in the full activity of childhood, halt as though an invisible hand had touched his shoulder, and stare? I remember such occasions in my own childhood, and in my manhood also, when a thing seen, which a moment ago was one of many and of no particular significance, has become singular, has separated itself from the stream of consciousness, and has become not an object but a source. What is the child staring at? Not at the flower or the drop of water or the face. The thing seen, which ordinarily halts our observation, has become not a wall but a window. The opaque has become the serene; he is looking through it… An artist is a child who stares, not at the imprisoning walls of life, but outward through the window.

The invisible hand is a visitation. Visitation from outside, from beyond, is a frequent theme in spiritual traditions. We might speculate as to the nature of the visitation, but there would be general agreement on two counts: it is mysterious and it is outside the power of the visited. Insofar as all these poems – in their original inspiration – come from somewhere beyond my control, a poem that is a response to a visitation might be considered a prayer, a prayer to the universe, or, as Teilhard de Chardin might suggest, a hymn to the universe.

A poetic sense is like a sixth sense. But that seems an inadequate description. I would be happier with a description that addressed the expansion of our already existing senses, and the way those senses interact and assist each other. In some of my poems I try to capture moments of sensual transition, periods – often brief and ephemeral – where one sense gives way to another, where two (or more) senses overlap or where they each refract different aspects of the same reality.

The poet is not some special creature existing in a rarefied sphere. He is part of the blood, sweat, tears and joy of life. Rilke described the place of the poet in his essay 'Concerning the Poet'. Sixteen oarsmen are rowing a boat upstream. The currents are strong; the task demanding. They pull as one, with outstretched arms, rising from their seats, meeting the forces of nature with determination and respect. One of the oarsmen, while continuing to play his part, sings a wordless song. His voice rises and falls. His singing arises out of the work and the strenuous camaraderie and in the listening the whole crew lift their eyes and look beyond.

Here, in *Excalibur's Return* and particularly in poems like 'Anglo Irish', 'Bad Language' and 'Offering a Poem to be Read', I draw attention to the music of words. The simple act of reading a poem out loud makes all the difference. It allows you not only to hear my voice more distinctly, but enables you to hear and to find your own. As I say in the latter poem, 'while I craft for the eye/I compose for the ear/so read at least once/out loud. Please.'

I also take you behind the scenes and give you a glimpse of the work that goes into making a poem. As Yeats said in 'Adam's Curse', we must labour to be beautiful. Sometimes the shortest poems are the longest in composition. They also may require more from you. They are so pared down, so spare and sparse, that if you don't bring a lot to the reading, they can appear meaningless.

To continue on our journey behind the scenes I would describe what I attempt to do when I write a poem like this: when you look straight ahead – without moving your eyes – what do you see to your right and left? A poem can offer you the opportunity to be aware of what is on the edge of consciousness. That is why the language of poetry is so often suggestive rather than instructive and the images of poetry, instead of informing, provoke.

Shakespeare was distressed by the ravages of time and how

it destroyed the beauty of the face he loved. In Sonnet 65 he asks how beauty – 'whose action is no stronger than a flower' – defends itself. Like Shakespeare, we can be brought close to despair. There is nothing we can do, 'unless,' as he says, 'this miracle have might/ That in black ink my love may still shine bright'.

This miracle is the poem he is writing. It is the poem we are reading. The words of the poem will forever speak the beauty of his love. A poem is no stronger than a flower, and yet, as Shakespeare says in Sonnet 19, 'my love shall in my verse ever live young.'

Creativity takes many forms. It does not always mean finding something new. It can be the re-finding of what has been lost; the re-discovery of what has always been at our side, but we have not slowed to stillness to make room for its presence. If 'Real Presence' made you pause, you will know what I'm talking about. Perhaps one of the pleasures of being older is the storehouse of memory is richer. There are greater opportunities for re-visitation, re-alignment and forgiveness.

When Morgan's invisible hand touches – and the touch is ever so light – there is nothing for it but to stop and stare and wait. A gift is being offered; a poem is announcing itself. The annunciation is non-verbal. The words send messengers ahead, scouts to read the lie of the land, to ascertain if you are in a state of profound, feminine receptivity. Some poems retreat at this stage or are soon aborted. Others implant. A word is formed, a note is struck, your flesh tingles, a scene appears before your eyes and away you go. Fun and games start up as alphabetical wonders appear and tantalisingly fade away. If we're lucky we snare them. Then we imprint the page: black on white.

I hope the act of reading poetry offers you a similar unpredictability and fun. If you are lucky, out of the ordinary something extraordinary may emerge. Who knows! It may be clothed in white samite! Be mystic, wonderful!